Broken Pieces
The Story Behind Gretta

Rhonda Whitaker

Kingdom Builders Publications LLC

© 2020 Rhonda Whitaker
Broken Pieces – The Story Behind Gretta
Kingdom Builders Publications, LLC

All rights reserved. No part of this book may be reproduced or transmitted in any form or by any means without written permission from the author.

Printed in the USA

ISBN 978-0-578-72555-0 Soft Cover
LCCN 2020912657

Authored by
Rhonda Whitaker

Editor
Wanda Brown
Louise James
Kingdom Builders Publications

Cover Design
LoMar Designs

Picture for cover

DEDICATION

I commit this book to God because He's brought me through so many things, and is still carrying me with His footprints.

I further dedicate this book to my children and grandchildren.

There are many people I can list, whom over the years have inspired me to write and publish this book but it is my children and grandchildren whom have encountered most of what's in this book from beginning to end.

To my biological sister, and my oldest daughter, who are one in the same. I took custody and raised her along with my children. She has been a great inspiration to my life in so many ways. She birthed two wonderful children whom have melted my heart away. My son, who taught me how to raise a man and gained a wonderful family with his spouse and a gorgeous grandson. To my daughter, who is the baby of the crew, but in many ways taught me the best way to become a great mother and grandmother. She and her spouse gave me three fantastic grandchildren. They are ALL my life and inspiration and I would take nothing for this journey.

Thanks for pushing me into the woman, mother, and grandmother I am today.

CONTENTS

	Dedication	iii
	Acknowledgement	v
1	Who is Gretta	1
2	Trouble in Paradise	8
3	Motion Sickness	18
4	Deep Waters	29
5	Understanding the Mission	41
6	The Distraction	44
7	Calling It Quits	50
8	Haunted By The Past	53
9	Dysfunctional Family	57
10	All The Way In	66
11	Sailing On Broken Pieces	72
12	In The City Now	76
13	Still Surviving	84
14	What's Next	91
	About the Author	100

ACKNOWLEDGMENTS

I acknowledge Elder Sylvia R. Whitaker for pushing me when I wanted to throw in the towel and just quit, for being a mother even in the times when you didn't understand how.

The Late Pastor Johnny Gilliam for giving me my first real prophecy which came to pass and still showing itself strong in my life, to Pastor Norman White who helped me to understand my gift and to give a platform to exercise my gift,

Pastor/Prophetess Cheryl Beaufort who I met in the DMV years ago who befriended me, mentored me, and loved me pass my pain, mistakes, and fears.

Pastor Elizabeth Gibson who prayed me through, even when I didn't want to keep going; when I didn't want to pray or keep on living. She was instrumental to help me see the real me; the one God saw.

Pastor Tyrone and Co-Pastor Nita Rose for allowing some of my gifts to be used, and for covering and praying for me.

Mrs. Louise Smith thanks for your gentle push and encouragement, you and I endured like good soldiers. Thank you for not giving up on my dream to become a writer. Thanks for pushing me into the creative world and bring out the writer in me while seeing me through the end of this road.

WHO IS GRETTA
Chapter One

Born 1975 in Manning, South Carolina, I grew up in Alcolu, South Carolina. Life was hard for me and Gretta, and that's the God's honest truth. Gretta is my alter ego and she always seem to find a way to get me in trouble! I was nice and meek, but Gretta was the wild one. When bad things happened to me or when I felt sad, Gretta always stepped in, but don't take my word for it. Keep reading, you'll see what I mean.

For as long as I can remember, my Grandma Kate was a strong force in my life. She was the apple of my eyes. Don't get me wrong, I loved my mom, but I was always with my grandma. We called her Mamo. She basically raised me and some of my other cousins as her own.

One day, when I was almost eight years old, I learned my dad, who I loved, appreciated, and adored, was not my real dad. That pierced my heart because I really loved him to pieces. I was told my real daddy did not want me because his family told him I did not belong to him. That was a heavy blow for a child to handle.

I grew up with most of what I needed but basically none of what I ever really wanted. I learned from a young age, life for me was going to be a struggle in many ways. When I was 8 years old, my mom developed a relationship with my real dad and they married in April of 1983. The real struggles began at this point; the point of my many broken pieces. The relationship changed between my mom and me once her husband came into the picture, and any chance for a good relationship with this man was nowhere in sight from the very beginning.

At the time, I had a three year old brother and was told I had another brother but had yet to meet him. I initially sensed my dad loved his alleged son more and didn't care about me, but I was wrong. The brother was a resident of Virginia, and so was dad, but dad was not a part of his life either, even though they both lived in Virginia before he and my mom got back together. I always wondered if my brother felt like me, neglected, and abandoned because our daddy proclaimed vehemently we were not his. I wondered whether it was just me who was abandoned. Dad typically was a reserved man. He was also a ticking time bomb which made it so hard to communicate with him. My dad was verbally abusive from the beginning and later became physically abusive to my mom, me, and my youngest brother. He was so abusive, I made a traumatic attempt to hurt him by hurting myself with drinking a glass of Clorox and some pills. My mom was pregnant with my sister. I was a desperate 12 year old when I failed at suicide.

We lived in a house not far from my grandmother Mamo's house. She had no idea what was going on. I was overwhelmingly scared of him. He was a habitual drugs and alcohol user. My mom still had to work while pregnant, because someone had to pay the bills. He was not responsible to keep the bare essentials going; we were often times in the dark. From my perspective, nothing was ever good enough for him; no matter what she tried to do. I thought about the time I tried an act of kindness so he might change his mind about me, and accept me. For a few years, Mamo had been teaching me how to cook. I had a bright idea to cook for mom and him so when my mom got home from a day's work, she would not have to cook. I just wanted her to come home and rest. This day, dad got home slightly before mom and asked, because of the dinner fragrance in the air, what was on the stove. I was careful to speak with a gentle pride, I made dinner. When I explained, he was abrupt and salty. He yelled at me about it then told me to never cook in his house again. He said, "That's what I have a wife for. I'm not going to eat your food." When mom arrived home from work, what started out as a heart-warming gesture, turned into a war of physical and verbal abuse. Because of this man's demented thoughts about me, he pushed my mom to the floor. She was about five months pregnant at the time. My intent was to make my parents happy, but this turned into a fiasco. That same night he told my mom he married her, not me and I was never to cook in his house again. I was completely traumatized.

This led me into years of silent frustrations. On this day, I just wanted him to die for his ill treatment he spewed on my family. My mom was a victim of his abuse in so many ways but never really spoke out against this villain, which villainized all of us. We were afraid we would be killed or see our mother killed, Mom was scared too, but would give us a false hope things would get better, and God was working it out for our good. I wasn't totally ignorant of what God could do, (because from an 11 year old young girl, I accepted God and received Him as my Lord and Savior), but admittedly, I questioned the crazy stuff going on in my life and the lives of MY immediate family. I have to say, I saw NO WAY OUT! I would dream, and daydream time and time again how I wanted my family to be like other families, but it seemed my wishes would never come true. There were always excuses why things were so wrong, but nothing was ever done to rectify and make the situation better at all; not even remotely.

At age eleven, I saw a new friend. She changed everything. Her name is Gretta; my friend/fiend inside. Gretta is my alter ego. She talked to me and enticed me to look at boys in a whole different light. She convinced me it was ok to start playing with boys. She was using me and I was using boys to cope with the demonizing lifestyle of my dysfunctional family. I didn't have friends as long as I could remember and could never understand why. I thought something was very wrong with me and was the reason other girls didn't liked me. My body was starting to change and everyone noticed, but not to compliment me. Some of the boys I hung out with would tell me some of the girls were mad at my physical development. They hated me because I had a nice shape and they were jealous of me. Deep down, I knew it was not true, but to fit in I just accepted it as truth and moved on. I started drowning myself with boy company because they paid attention to me; even though it was for all the wrong reasons. An eleven-year-old cannot comprehend that. I became someone other people in my family could never be proud of but at the time the boys gave me attention I never got from anywhere else. I was gullible to any and everything they said to me. Boys were my hiding place. I learned the gateway to sex and hid myself there. I swam and drowned daily in sexual activities along with other schemes to get through the smothering feelings of hopelessness of an absent love from my family.

I never felt pretty or happy about whom I'd become. Nobody once ever told me I was fearfully and wonderfully made by God and He loved me. Even though I received the God ideal, nobody ever taught me God's Word, nor did I investigated it for myself. I'm not sure about God, but I certainly felt like an outsider in my family. When at our family reunions, I was an outcast. I noticed the difference but never reconciled I was chosen. I learned decades later God had a great call on my life, but at that susceptible age, you just consider yourself awkward, and thought it was a part of life to be ostracized by family members which made it okay for others to do the same. So often we hear the term black sheep in families. I heard my mom say she was the black sheep of her family. I felt the same way, not really understanding the meaning; just by the name itself, I thought, me too. I lived under a cloud with this idiom I would never accomplish anything or get anything right like my younger sister. I was treated indifferently. I had no one to look up to, everyone appeared to live for themselves, nor did anyone seem to notice what was going on with me. I resounded the alarms of my brokenness for the right kind of attention, but kept attracting the attention of outsiders and men who gave me a false reality of feel-good. I needed to feel like somebody, if but only for a little while.

Since I was a young girl, I had a gift to see and interpret dreams. I was clairvoyant and could see things and people. I, though, wondered about my own life, my own dreams, if my dreams or visions would come true. Eventually, I surmised they would never come true. I rebelled with sex, boys, and phone sex as my insatiable outlet. in retrospect, although I felt unloved and unwanted, thank God for having His hands on me. My story did not destroy me. I yet stand because I know I should've been dead.

TROUBLE IN PARADISE
Chapter Two

By age 11, I experienced many kinds of sicknesses and deaths in my life. I was tried and tested with illnesses which should have killed me. God had his hands on me from the beginning and every experience I've battled was well worth it. Those experiences made me the woman of God I am today.

In 1989, I was 14 years old, I was focused and all I wanted to do was get an education, but sickness became a big part of my life. I was in and out of hospitals, with one diagnosis after another. This happened after my parents moved to Newport News, Virginia. . At first the move seemed so wrong. I felt inferior and unloved by my parents. The true devastation was being pulled farther away from my grandmother. Mamo was my advocate. She was the only person whose love I could feel. I had a long-standing playmate relationship with suicide. Following years of feeling taunted by family and outsiders I battled in my mind whether dying would be better than living. Later, I got into a new school and was getting the hang of it, but became ill again. I was reduced to homebound schooling. My supposedly predictable routines where turning in to something else. The unpredictable routines were the new normal. For as sure as we settled into this routine, something bad happened.

I was in the fourth week of isolation with home schooling, which meant I was hidden and most likely forgotten. This one mid-morning, I decided to get some air from my porch when I saw some girls. I thought they could be potential friends. I walked closer toward their direction. Two of the girls pulled away quickly, but one drew to me. Little by little, we developed a friendship. We got to know each other in a matter of a few months. I could finally say I had a best friend. I did return to class at school to finish out the year. When my middle school year was over, I was excited to head to high school. Home life was still a struggle, so I stayed outside from after school until dark most days. I didn't receive harassment at school and I felt more love from my friend's house than I did at my own.

On this particular day in school, I could hardly wait to get home from school. That afternoon, for some reason, was very different. I went inside my house and watched television waiting for mom to get home from work. I needed to spend some time with her. She got into her customary duty of preparing dinner.

She didn't have time to really talk to me like I needed her to. She wasn't paying me as much attention as I needed. I was an invisible presence in the room. It didn't work out for me nevertheless, I decided to go outside. I reckoned I needed to be by myself to talk and think. By myself was where I found peace and time to myself to think about the many things going on in my life. I had some change I found in my room earlier, and hope some friends would be close by. No one was out there so I went through the hoop, as we called it. The "Hoop" was the area we walked through for a shortcut to the neighborhood store. This afternoon seemed to be no different than any other. When I got through the hoop, this man approached me. He demanded I open my legs as he pushed me to the side of a wall of the building between some bushes. I thought about my life ending that very moment and no one was around to help me escape. In total fear for my life, if I didn't do what he said. I'm thinking, "Where was Gretta when I needed her?" as he forced himself inside me, I remembered I had some homemade pepper spray in my pocket. My friend Tina told me she carries it around for protection. So I reached for it while he tried to penetrate me. I sprayed as hard as I could into his eyes and he fell back. I ran as fast as I could to get home into my room alone, never to repeat what had just happened again. It was the longest night in silence. I couldn't tell anyone what had happen to me, not even my friend. I felt responsible for what happened. I dare not tell my parents. They would have agreed with me and blamed me for what happened.

It was so hard keeping these lies inside. I wanted to confide in my mother, but she was going through her own issues. She dealt with domestic violence, drugs, drinking as well as verbal abuse. I didn't have the heart to add one more thing to her already volatile life. My dad was a handful. It was hard enough dealing with him with his eruptive state. Our home was not pleasant, safe, comfortable, friendly, or good to me. We lived inside a thick wall and was stuck; not able to share our feelings, thoughts, love, or heartfelt wishes. I felt as if we were voided creatures and our cries would not be honored because we were ALL closet liars. Our home was broken because all the hurt my mom and I experienced. Not to mention, during this same time, I was being touched by family members. I wondered why my mom never noticed something was wrong. I used to feel hurt because she never noticed something was wrong with me. You would think your own mom would notice something was off with her own child. I didn't have the courage to tell her, I just kept hoping for the day my mom would notice something was wrong. That day never came. I just became my own personal company; staying to myself and bottled up all my problems inside. This was all making me a very bitter person. I built walls to keep from being cut any deeper. No one loved, cared or, saw what I dealt with on the inside. I certainly wasn't going to let them into my real truth.

My dad's mom would take me to her house a lot when she wasn't working, and would show me how to cook her favorite meals. I was grateful because this took a lot off my mind. However, couldn't reveal my pinned-up life because I was afraid she would tell my mom and dad and I would be in trouble. Church was another safe haven. I sang in the choir and danced with the praise dance team, but on the inside I was plagued with fear, hurt and neglect. I kept questioning why my parents couldn't see I was messed up? They didn't, they just kept going on like nothing was wrong. I used to tell myself I would never let my children, if I ever had any, go through the things I went through.

When I was about 15, my mom sent me and my brother back to South Carolina to live with my Mamo. Mom kept my sister with her because she was too young to come with us. We were in school. I was a full-time parent to my younger brother. Our mom was over 300 miles away going through hell with her husband. We got a call saying mom was in the hospital having surgery. When she returned home from the hospital, dad threw a full beer can and hit her in the head after an argument. Although I wasn't there, I hoped he could feel my rage and contempt. Our hate was tantamount. I have a similar contempt for my mom because she received the abuse, and dad because he gave the abuse.

Dealing with my low self-esteem, my mom's abuse, our abuser, and the care of my brother, I would sneak boys into my Mamo's house and let them do whatever they wanted to do. It was the only attention I was getting, and Gretta convinced me it was ok. I started dating a guy from high school who played sports, and we talked a lot on the phone but hardly saw each other. Even though we were in this relationship, I wondered if he was like the next guy; playing over me. Who did I have in my life to teach me how to love or be loved? Who was going to show me how to be a teenager, especially with all the things I was dealing with? I was a whore and that was my truth. I was drawn to whomever paid me the slightest bit of attention.

My parents moved back to Carolina in 1991, so I went to live with them from Mamo's house. In the summer, when I was 16, we had some new neighbors move in and it was a big family. One of the sons talked to me more because we were closer in age and were classmates. By the time the new school started back, I skipped my interest to the oldest son, Allen. I wanted to be with him. Allen treated me sweet and gentle, and told me I was a beautiful person. He appeared to really care a lot for me. As time went by, I saw his words reciprocated his actions. We dated for over one year before he even attempted to touch me. He showed me something different and I respected him for it.

We're back in school but we had to be a secret couple. His daddy was not going for that. However, his mom vouched and rooted for us to be together. she say she wanted me to be her daughter-in-law. She went on to say, I was perfect for her son and she knew he loved me. She repeated his words of love, how he talked to her about me all the time, he was in love with me, and one day I would become his wife. Allen was older than me, so his daddy didn't want to hear anything about it, he certainly didn't want to hear about me. So we had a "fly on the wall" love affair. We kept things on the down low.

The first time we were intimate with each other was nothing like the other guys. He was gentle with me and showed me consideration and care. Before I knew what happened, the relationship came to an end. Without warning or explanation, Allen started pulling away from me, My rebellious nature kicked in and I started talking to other people. We seemed to be spending more time apart than together. I used to being hurt so I took it like a champ. It was no different from what everyone else had done to me. How many guys would I allow to just use me for sex, or say the four letter word but didn't really mean it?

I was told I would never be anything or amount to anything, so I became comfortable acting the part. I was now in 12th grade. I'd been with so many guys until I lost count. I was with guys who went to school with me, guys from my church, and guys from the community. Honestly, I turned to sex to feel like I was someone I really wasn't. I was never taught how to be a young lady and told men were supposed to respect me. Most of my life I witnessed my mom being abused. One day I decided I was not going to just let men sleep with me and I needed to learn how to respect myself.

I started working at Piggly Wiggly in Manning to be able to purchase items needed for graduation. I didn't purchase school portraits because we could not afford them. Along with wanting self-worth, I worked because I wanted to go to cosmetology school. I battled with my hair throughout school and was teased.

Everything I did, growing up, was so I could fit in, but it never seemed to work. The only thing I had going was scoring with guys. I realized the only reason boys talked to me was to get the goods. That was high school. College life could be better because my goals would be different. I saw me as a full-time college student and a working-class girl. Things needed to change.

I frequented church very often. There was a guy who came to worship sporadically. His name was Calvin. When Calvin came, he would look at me all the time and he would send words through his cousin to tell me. He started sending letters by his cousin. He wanted me to know he liked what he saw and wanted to get to know me. After a few months, he worked up the nerve to talk to me one Sunday after church. We exchanged phone numbers. I don't know what he saw and I don't know what he heard, but we started a relationship. It wasn't the best circumstance, because he lived in Sumter and I lived in Alcolu, which was about a 20 mile distance. I saw him more regularly in church. One Sunday, we got the ok for him to come over after church and make our relationship official. We were together for a while when he decided to move to Alcolu. We saw each other more often because of his cousins and aunt. Our relationship blossomed. Once I graduated, I considered myself an adult. I picked Calvin up and we spend the full day together. Before my parents came home, I took him back to his home.

I started college and things seemed to be going great. However, one Sunday, Calvin and I had an encounter. Things got turned up after an argument at church. It was our first argument and it was our public disagreement. I found out he was talking to other women. I disrespected my mom's curfew just to be with him. I had even gone to hotels with him and not coming home. One day my mom and I argued about it and she told me since I could not obey her rules, (even though I was grown), I had to move out of her house. No worries! I moved in with my Mamo. After which, my mom told me Calvin's mom said I wasn't good enough for her son. It felt like a ton of bricks – that hurt a whole lot, which explains why he started acting even more different with me. It was no longer feasible to continue the relationship, so we broke off it off.

MOTION SICKNESS
Chapter Three

Now Calvin had moved on. I decided to move to Sumter with my best friend, go to school, and start over. Three weeks after moving with my friend I met a man named Mark who was ten years my senior. At the time I was 18. I was an adult, so age didn't matter. After meeting Mike, things progressed quickly. We were getting to know each other more and more every day. As time passes, I started feeling sick. I did not know what was going on with my body. From a young age, doctors told my mom I would never have children because of a twisted uterus and endometriosis, so I just thought I was homesick or had a bad stomach virus. The thought of being pregnant never crossed my mind.

Mom contacted me through one of my cousins ask me to come back home to stay. I wondered why she wanted me back home after disobeying her house rules. After all, she told me to leave. I knew deep within, my mom loved me very much, but her ability to show it was crippling to us both. I had a problem with her letting her husband talk to her any kind of way; she never stood up for herself. I felt some kind of way. I sat and watched how she was abused in many ways, but mostly verbal and mental abuse. Now I was a grown woman, seeing how she allowed herself to be treated caused me to lose a lot of respect for her. Things happened to me and I thought she should have recognized them because I was her daughter. I was touched by men in my family, but I kept it all balled up on the inside because I didn't feel no one really loved or cared for me. Most times I didn't want to live, I just wanted to die. What was the real reason for living? Nobody loved me or cared for me. I didn't even like myself. I was so alone, invisible, and lost.

Nevertheless, I did move back home. once I returned home, I started having nausea, vomiting, and back pain, and extra tiredness. I still commuted to Sumter every day for school. I rode with my cousin and my auntie to school. I got out of class two to three hours before them on most days, so I went to Mark's house until they picked me up. While continuing this relationship and getting to know each other more, I was getting sicker. I decided to walk to the drug store to get some pain pills for my back because the pain was getting worse every day. The back pain got so bad until I took the pills and went to bed every day I got home from Sumter. About two weeks later, I noticed my breasts were feeling tender, so I talked to my dad about it first. I was hesitant and afraid to talk to my mom, especially after moving back home and we hadn't had a real conversation yet. My dad said he didn't know what was going on with me, but I needed to talk to my mom. I was still too afraid to talk with her so I told him I would do it the next day.

When I got home from school the next day, mom in her bedroom ironing clothes for the week. This was something she did for years. as I entered her room, I caught her eye staring at me. I didn't dignify her look, just knelt at the foot of her bed. She caught me by surprise. All other times I needed her line of questioning for my sad estate, I would not get, so imagine my astonishment when she asked, "What's wrong?" I went in soft by saying, "I'm having all of these symptoms with back pain and my breast." She came back with a look and a tone and said, "You need to go to the doctor. I think you are pregnant. I have been watching you and your skin is very pretty lately."

I looked, listened, and trembled on the inside, not knowing what was next. I did not want to believe what she was saying, because I was told I couldn't bear children. I previously had a miscarriage with my former boyfriend. That was the full extent of our conversation.

When I finished classes at school the following day, my boyfriend came for me, and I suggested we have a long talk. We went to the drug store and bought two pregnancy tests. I waited until morning to take them because I heard people say it was better to use your first morning urine to get accurate results. When I tested the first time after three minutes, it showed positive. I told myself, "Oh that's a lie!" I took the second test and within the first minute the test proved positive again. "Oh my God! It's true. I really am pregnant!" I had no inkling of what to do. The real love of my life, Calvin walked away from me, the relationship I presently in is with the father of my baby, was excruciating because I really didn't love him. He was a pest. I had some type of feeling for him, but he was not my ex. the very next day after school, I went over to my baby's daddy house and told him I was indeed pregnant. He thought it was good but in my mind I'm saying, "I made a big mistake because I wanted Calvin back!" Now I having another man's baby; how will that work out?

I had a short fling after Calvin, but before Mark. His name was Ron. I wondered if the baby I'm carrying could be his baby. We started hanging together and going out. He was more serious than I. He desired to be with me all the time. He wanted me to meet his family and friends. He was a very kind, sweet, compassionate man. I liked being with him and going out with him because he showed me a lot of attention. Momentarily, I needed that in my life. He was very gallant; opening doors, pulling my chair, and other chivalrous gesture. He took me out and purchased whatever I wanted. I was not in love with him but cared for him and admittedly, he shared the same feelings. We decided to cultivate a relationship after being with each other. However, after a few months, I realized I made a mistake. He was not the person I wanted to be with, plus I had gone back to talking with Calvin again. As Calvin and I continued to communicate. I almost confident we would get back together, so I distanced myself from Ron by ignoring his calls and pretending I was not at home when he came by, I got Mamo to participate in the lie if he came there to see me, she was instructed to tell him I was not home.

All though I was in several relationships, I still frequented the church and got more involved. I became president of the young adult choir at my church while being flirtatious with different men at the same time. I was at a point in my life where I used men to feel like I was a part of somebody, if only for a little while. I had become who I said I would never become, but it was something about the attention I craved, I didn't just want it, I needed it. I grew up not feeling loved, so men showing me some attention made me feel good for a moment.

Once I realized I did not want to be with Ron anymore, the same thing happened with Calvin and he continued his relationships with other women. In fact, he had a baby from the woman he was seeing at the time. That information did a real number on me. I sunk into depression. There was nothing I could do with that, so I moved on. I was hurt, used, broken, and abused. I couldn't be mad; I was using them too for my insatiable appetite fulfillments.

I told Mark I was going to have his child. He turned up the clinginess. his efforts were in vain. I was still in love with Calvin. When I got home late evening, I told my mom I was pregnant. She told me she knew it and I needed to go to the doctor. I followed up the next day. The doctor said I was almost seven weeks pregnant and the baby was due around October 8th of that year.

It was time to face my family and the world. I was almost 19 years old. I knew my family would show a lot of negativity towards my mom and me. My mom was considered the black sheep of her family. She was ostracized, ridiculed, and excluded from many family events. What makes a family travel to visit relatives from another state, but make a point not to visit the house of a significant family member? Some of the family did not like her husband and didn't care for her children. This was why mom felt so broken and left out. When my mom's family found out I was pregnant, some of them had very adverse things to say, but I did not let it bother me. People are quick to judge and forget the things they did. God lets us know there are no little or big sin, they are all the same in His sight. Some of my relatives were living with their boyfriends and weren't married, but had the nerve to condemn me.

When the body goes through a change or a health challenge, you will automatically be attuned; feeling suspicious of anything you could find going wrong. I was growing rapidly. My secret will soon be out because I could not hide the pregnancy for much longer. Repeatedly, the baby's daddy kept getting on my nerves. He is a clinger. He called all the time. It got to the place where we changed our house number. He took harassment to a whole new level. When I went to class any given day, he would stand outside all day waiting on me to come out. It got so bad, I had to ask my professor to ask him to leave the premises. Even though I was still seeing him, I just needed a break because he was nagging me about everything. When he would call the house, I would use my brother and sister to tell him things, but it did not seem to work. We went to the movies. I used my siblings as decoys in hopes he would not touch or bother me as much. Well, that plan failed because while sitting in the movies, he was the same nagging octopus as when we had no company or in a public place. He kept putting his arm around me and kissing me. Nothing seemed to change in his mind.

I knew I had to get out of this relationship. On a Sunday morning, I invited him to church and dinner at my house so we might talk about the baby and our relationship. I worked up the nerve to tell him I was done. Of course, he did not take the news well. Then to exacerbate matters, he began stalking me. He called multiple times every day and night. I told my parents about his behavior and my mom tried talking to him, but nothing seemed to work. Every day I went to school, I had to deal with him asking for me. He even came on the hair floor. I think he tried to get me kicked out. However, no matter what he did, I still did not want anything to do with him. I assured him he could be in his baby's life, but the relationship between us was over.

Finally, after giving Mark the cold shoulder, he got the message and moved on. Calvin was now trying to get back into my life. Initially, I was cold towards him because he hurt me. I wanted him to think I didn't want him anymore, while deep inside, I screamed YES!

A few months went by. I was on the phone with Calvin when suddenly, I felt extremely sick. I was only 4 ½ months pregnant when I was diagnosed with pre-eclampsia and was placed on bed rest for the rest of the pregnancy. Although Calvin and I spent lots of time on the phone, but in person, something wasn't right between us. I had this premonition and I knew something was fishy. As suspected, he was seeing another young lady who went to one of the churches where we fellowshipped. Calvin's cousin was dating one and he was dating the other.

Bed rest was hard. I tried to concentrate on my child growing on the inside of me. I prayed God would help me make it through the last two months of pregnancy. I was completely absent of love, trust and the whole nine with family members and my choice of men. Which was worse?

Dad made me feel fatherless and unloved. Living with him was a hellacious set of events. It was the summer of my pregnancy. Every day my mom went to work, he turned off the air and used a fan for himself alone. I would be in bed smoldering from the heat. He'd turn the air on shortly before mom got home so the house would cool, she would not suspect his evil deed. He was just mean and insufferable. I had it bad on the inside and the outside.

On the one hand, I was a woman, maturing into a mother, while on the other, I was treated like an orphan. To make matters worse, he would not talk to me or ask if I was hungry. Who treats their own child like that? Many times, I wished myself dead. I wished I had never been born. Whether it was school, home, church, or family Abandoned was my name. Talking to anyone about it was out of the question because who was going to listen? Who would take me to a medical specialist to sit and talk about my problems? I was afraid of asking anyone for anything. I lived with silent frustration.

I was admitted to the hospital days before my baby was born. I was very sick. At a point, the doctors wanted me to have emergency surgery. My grandmother used to talk to me saying when it was time for my baby to come, I should have a natural birth. I decided to have the baby naturally, without medicine. the nurses tried to talk me into having an epidural. My grandmother was right, I held to my guns and denied the medicine.

After having my new baby boy, he was sick and so was I. I needed a blood transfusion immediately. I was in the hospital for almost a week then I started feeling better. Baby and I were released on Halloween night; I will never forget it. I was going home as a new mother but confident and comfortable because I helped raise two of my siblings.

When my maternity leave was over, I found a babysitter for my son and returned to school. The babysitter was the aunt of my ex-boyfriend, Calvin. He was living with her so he saw me and my son every day which allowed us to reacquaint. I was very careful because he had hurt me so many times before and I was not going to allow him to hurt me again. I needed to keep my mind focused on being a new mom and college.

I let Calvin back in my life. We were fully back; loving as we were from the beginning. Wow, the love of my life was back with me and I felt the world was revolving and I was loving it!

DEEP WATERS
Chapter Four

November 1994 changed my life forever. Calvin and I discussed marriage, but never told anyone about it. We had a friend from church who agreed to take us to the courthouse. So, one day, without anyone knowing, we got married in Manning, S.C. It was a pretty cut and dry ceremony. Our only witness, besides the probate judge and his secretary, was my 10-month-old son. I will never forget it, because we were married with nowhere to go or no place to stay. Calvin was living with a friend from church and I was living at home, but we were legally husband and wife. Soon after, Calvin left his friend's house and went back to Sumter to live with his mom. He later he got sick with a cold and was down in the bed. His mom sent for me. She told Calvin, "Since you have a wife, she needs to take care of you." Immediately, I moved in with my husband which I was grateful for. We had man issues and moving in with his mom did not solve the many problems we had. I needed a way to get to school. Calvin was not working and we only had a AID to FAMILIES AND DEPENDANT CHILDREN (AFDC) and some food stamps. His mom wanted us to be responsible for making sure food was in the house and to pay the water bill.

I could not understand why my husband would get jobs but not work any of them for more than a few weeks. Well, I finally realized he was lazy. He always had an excuse for why the jobs didn't work out and it was never his fault. So with the both of us being home and him not working, caused problems between us. We were mad at each other more than we were happy. Don't get me wrong, I loved my husband but he just would not stay on a job. My father-in-law even got him hired at his job. He didn't keep that job either, more excuses!

As the months went by, I noticed some kicks in my stomach, cravings, and my menstrual cycle was off. On Thanksgiving Day, I had a conversation with mom about the kicks in my stomach. She told me one of my cousins visiting was a nurse and I should speak to her. My cousin called me into the bedroom and touched my stomach. She instantly said, "You are pregnant. You need to go to the doctor as soon as possible."

Monday morning, my husband and I went to the doctor. I took a pregnancy test and we waited. When the doctor came in to speak with us about the test, he said, "I have some good news and I have what could be bad news. Yes, you are pregnant, but it seems like you are at least 5 and a half months pregnant. I'm sending you over to the hospital ASAP because you need an immediate ultrasound."

We went to the hospital for the ultrasound and returned to the doctor's office as advised. The doctor started explaining to my husband and me I was indeed pregnant and about 5 months along. There were concerns about the baby. The doctor scheduled an appointment for us to have a chorionic villus sampling done in Columbia, SC. The doctor said the baby's organs were not developing and she would most likely be born with many difficult medical problems which would take a toll on her life. I was placed me on strict bed rest immediately and a nurse would be scheduled to come to the house and monitor both the baby and me. I was warned she may not make full term and if she did, it could be a bigger danger for both her and me. I was told her kidneys were not forming, her brain was not forming, and she only had a few fingers and toes. I was really scared.

I was monitored closely because my blood pressure was high and I had a lot of blood leaking into my urine. One day while home by myself, I started bleeding so heavily until I called the doctor. He told me to come to the hospital immediately to be admitted. After being admitted, the doctor gave me a little while to have the baby on my own, but because of the pre-eclampsia, my blood pressure was rising and the baby's heartbeat was declining. The Doctor prepared to have me airlifted to Columbia for an emergency surgery. I prayed because I wanted a natural birth just like my first one. I did not want an epidural and I didn't want to be cut.

My prayers were answered. I had my baby where I was; thank God. My new baby girl was here! However, before I could get happy at small victories, the doctor said my baby girl might have to be transported to Richland Memorial Hospital if they were unable to perform procedures needed to save her little life. She was already 2.5 months early and extra small. She was given a fifty-fifty chance of survival. I was so scared and didn't know anything else to do but pray until something changed. Thank God she did not have to be transported to Columbia.

After having my baby girl, I was unable to see her or hold her because they had to rush her to emergency surgery. I wondered with worry and panic, what would happen to my baby? Would she live or would she die? I had to leave fearful thinking and proclaim God's word and believe she would live a full and healthy life. Three days later, I was released to go home but my very small little angel had to stay in the hospital. She needed help breathing, she needed a brain procedure, and special formula to help her grow enough before she could be released.

For three long weeks my daughter was in the hospital in Manning, SC and I had to go up there three times a day to see her and breast feed her because this would be the best way to help her gain weight and grow.

After 33 days, we received news she could come home but we had to stay close because she would have multiple doctor visits a week. Commuting to Manning so many times a week from Sumter would be a great challenge, so we stayed with my parents. Much sooner than later, our baby girl was getting stronger and we could return home to Sumter.

We've had our issues with everything which goes along with staying with mom, dad, the baby, and Calvin, and now we're back at our very own stomping ground. Settling in, things were starting to look up. Nonetheless, about a week later, non-stop bleeding occurred, I wound up at the doctors three to four times a week. They tried different types of procedures, but nothing seemed to help.

After being home just two months with my new baby girl, learning to care for her special needs, and taking care of my 18-month-old son, I was met with the challenge of leaving them for a serious operation at such a young age… I had to have an emergency hysterectomy. At the time of the surgery, they discovered again with child, about 8 weeks along. The devastation to lose this fetus was daunting, but the baby would not have survived for nine months, so it was unavoidable to end the pregnancy during the emergency hysterectomy. I had to be cut the old-fashioned way because they could not do it vaginally.

After a week in the hospital, I was discharged and it was the happiest thing to me. I was sad about the baby I lost in the surgery, but was happy I was alive to be with my husband, my son, and baby girl.

My second day home, I was racked with so much pain. Calvin called the doctor to see if this was normal. The doctor told me what to do but if I weren't any better by morning, I should return to the hospital. I returned for four more days due to an infection. They had to dissolve the issue by placing a small whole in my abdomen for drainage for several days and give me antibiotics.

Once better, I was discharged to recover at home. I knew life was going to be challenging caring for small children. My mom and dad took my son for a while until I got better. So he was in Manning with them for a few months so I could heal.

Things were going well, but if my husband would just stay on a job, things could be better. I felt like the man and the woman because I was doing everything. I recovered from a major medical situation, running the household, and caring for the children. I was raised to believe marriage is sacred and one should be the helpmate to the husband, so I wasn't going to quit because of hard times. We maintained through the struggles and got through, though it all fell on me. I went to my mom for help even though we lived with his mom.

His mom kept a roof over our heads but the price for this small comfort was high. We went through hell and high water, low water, and no water for it. There were several times, I wanted to pack my children up and disappear. Nevertheless, I promised to hold on for my them.

The next couple of years went by and we moved back to Manning and got our own place. We first got a small house in Alcolu, across the street from my grandmother's house and then we moved to Manning Lane Apartments. Once we were in Manning Lane Apartments things really started to digress. It was as if we were going downhill on a daily basis.

Eventually, we met a man in Manning who was a cleaning contractor. He had a contract to clean a brake plant. He allowed us to become sub-contractors for him and we made a lot of money. We were able to take care of our home and children like we needed to. During this time, 1997, my mom offered to have us a real wedding because we were married in the courthouse in 1994. Things had changed tremendously for us in so many ways. Even though these great things were happening for us, I was sick.

One morning in 1997, my husband was on jury duty and I was at home with the children. I was babysitting my God-son. While rocking him to sleep, my nose started bleeding. No matter what I did to stop it, it continued to bleed. I called the doctor's office which was right up the street. They told me to come in immediately, and I did. They used a syringe to inject a liquid medicine up my nose and allowed me to lay there for thirty minutes to monitor the situation. After thirty minutes, I went home.

About twenty minutes after getting home, my nose started bleeding again, and this time it was worse. No matter what I did, it just bled and bled. Holding my head back, holding a cold cloth on my nose; and other known remedies didn't help. No matter what I tried, it just bled and bled. This time when I called the doctor's office, they told me to go to the emergency room. I waited on my god-son's mom to pick him up. She went to the courthouse to tell my husband I was being rushed to the hospital.

Once I was there, they put cold ice on me and squirted medication up my nose, but to no avail. Nothing was working. I was rushed to get a cat scan but before I could get in the machine, I screamed for help and blacked out. When I woke up so many nurses and doctors were working on me from head to toe. All I could see was a white light. I just wanted my mom. I started praying because I heard someone say, "She is losing too much blood and we need to get it stopped or she will be in a world of trouble."

I was transported to an Orangeburg Hospital where I stayed for about three weeks. I had to have a surgery without putting me to sleep because it was too dangerous. By this time, I was asking the nurse if I was going to die because I was choking on my own blood; blood they could not get to stop. I was hemorrhaging and I thought, this is it; I'm going to die. No family was around for support. I was alone and scared. I was in so much pain, weak, and afraid of what was going to happen to me. I had a brain aneurism. I was hospitalized for three weeks.

After three or four blood fusions, and feeling a little stronger, I was released to go home. I wasn't well enough to climb the stairs for bed; I couldn't walk without assistance, or bathe on my own. I needed help with everything. Calvin was finally working and our son was in the head start program, so I was home all day with my baby girl. My neighbor would drop in to help and make sure I got something to eat. I was not feeling my strongest. It was taking a long time to heal because my hemoglobin was below the normal range, but it was coming up very slowly. One night out of despair and desperation, I called my parents to our house. I wanted to talk to them and my husband about taking care of my children because I did not want to live like this anymore. I was weak, depressed, and couldn't do much for myself. I had to wait for people to do everything for me and I hated it. My mom immediately ministered to me saying things would get better.

I turned to the wall and went to sleep around 3:30

a.m. I woke up and wondered why God didn't take me home. It would be better than what I was presently going through. When I realized God didn't let me to die, I asked Him why would He let me go through all this stuff. He responded to me in a dream saying, I made a promise to Him the year before which was to be His disciple and go into ministry. He called me and I said yes. I kept saying I was going to do it, but never did. In the dream I was standing in pulpits and praying. People were slayed in the Spirit without me ever touching them.

I knew what the dream meant, so the next day I found strength enough to pray. I promised God when He healed my body, I would do the work He called me to do. God showed himself strong and healed my body, yet again.

One Friday night, mom took me to a worship service our family had not far from my house. The man preaching was a very good friend and we attended his ministry often. He was a powerful pastor we'd grown to love. He told mom to bring me to the revival he was holding this night because he wanted to lay hands on me and pray. He said he could see in the Spirit the devil was trying to take me out. So my mom called me and told me to be ready. Calvin helped me dress.

After getting to the service, I felt the power of love in the church. The pastor called my name, walked over to me, and prayed for me. Instantly, I felt strength in my body. When the service was over, the pastor laid hands on me again and prayed for me. He said God was calling me to a higher place, and I had a work to do for God. He said I needed to heed to God's word. I went home with more strength in my body than I'd had when I got there. This made me feel better. I thought a lot about what the pastor said. I knew I had not done what God had called me to do.

UNDERSTANDING THE MISSION
Chapter Five

Slowly but surely, I began feeling better. I was grateful God was healing me and I continued to trust and believe Him. I was tired of running from my calling, so I spoke with my pastor telling him about the calling on my life. He said he could see the calling on my life and encouraged me to do what God was calling me to do.

My initial sermon was scheduled for November 1999. The sermon was done to become a minister of the Gospel. I made a vow to God no matter what came my way, I would do His will. I told the Lord I would preach His word in and out of season- when folk wanted to hear it and when they did not. I was finally ready to do the things for God which would make Him smile and be happy with my life.

While I made the commitment to serve God with the call on my life, I didn't feel I had the support of my husband. Instead of joining me, he complained of me being in church all the time and not spending time with him. I understood the balanced life, and I spent time with my husband. I took care of my motherly and wifely duties; in fact, I went above and beyond to make sure my wifely duties were done.

Calvin was absent even while he was present. I felt alone at times. I screamed for help on the inside but nobody saw the signs. I felt those closest to you should be sensitive enough to tell when something is wrong. I could not understand why no one saw my warning signs. Why must I always have to say something when I was in trouble? I could tell if something was wrong by facial expressions, body language or just by the way a person was acting. I was so in-tuned with my family, my children would often ask me how did I know things without them telling me? I told them, "When you get older and get to know your loved ones, you'll understand their personalities. You don't always need words to tell you when something is wrong."

Who did I have to lean on, to talk to, and share my feelings with? Who was going to tell me it was going to be ok? Who was going to say to me, "I'm sorry you are going through this?"

I experienced these feelings of being alone throughout my life, but I thought once I was married, things would be different, but they weren't. I finally realized I had to go through certain experiences because of the call God placed on my life. I knew from a child I was a prophet called, anointed, and appointed by God and I had to endure what others didn't have to endure. I had to see things unfamiliar to others and to battle wars because I was built to fight. With God, the battle was already won, however, I had to show the Devil even though he worked through others to take me down, I would still win the war.

I used to dream I fought wars for others through sickness, pain, and other tests. However, in real life, God has everything in His hands. I know He will always strengthen me and with Him I will win. So, the battle was on, and I promised God I was in it to win it. So the real question was what was next?

THE DISTRACTION
Chapter Six

One month later, in December 1999, It was as if I was living in a hurricane. My husband and I argued all the time over simple stuff, like who left the cap off the toothpaste. The fact he still couldn't keep a job didn't help either. As long as things went his way, he was fine. However, there was a price to pay if things did not go his way. Calvin wanted to have his cake and eat it too. Don't get me wrong, I was not miss perfect, but why did we have to argue about simple things? He especially didn't like me going to church during the week. He would say I was in church too much. I told him he found me in church, so I wasn't about to stop for no one, not even him. We seem to be pulling away from each other more and more, but I felt church kept me sane. I was the mommy and pulling the slack of the daddy role, and all the income came from me. My husband could get jobs, but he just wouldn't keep them. I found out after two or three weeks on a job, he'd tell a lie about my health so he wouldn't have to go back. I learned one time he told his boss I had a tumor on the brain. Early on, I wasn't aware he was telling these lies. What man is so lazy to lie on his wife's health to quit his job so his wife would have to make the ends meet? What man is okay with the wife keeping a roof over his head while he lounges around all day long?

While there were many things my mom did not teach me, she did teach me how to be a good wife to my husband. I was a good wife and I was a hard worker. We ended up in and out of homes because of employment and money issues. I suffered many illnesses, but most times, I had to forget about what I was dealing with and just made myself go to work.

I did what I had to do to keep my family going. I was a high school graduate, went to beauty school, got my phlebotomist license, but at one point, I was a greeter in Food Lion in my hometown. I was trained as a cashier because I needed more money to take care of the family.

At the same time, I was being cheated on! I was told my van was seen at unusual places. I looked into the allegations and discovered my husband was cheating on me. How was I going to deal with being cheated on and continue to make the children feel like everything was ok? My husband and I decided to move to Atlanta to get a fresh start. My parents kept the children until we got settled. A few months later, we returned to get the children. My mother's child; my biological sister became my daughter. In order for her to move to Atlanta with me to go to school, my parents had to sign her over to me. She had lived with me, so now it was time to make it official. We all moved in with some friends who were helping us out until we could get on our feet.

Everything was good at first, but too many people living under one roof can wind up failing at some point. Goodness can't last forever. We moved into a hotel room and paid by the week until we could find our own place to stay. Every weekend, we commuted South and then back to Atlanta just in time for the children to get to school and for me to get to work. We did this weekly.

We got a place and things were looking up, again. Less than a month later, my brother-in-law and his son came from South Carolina to stay with us. A deeper responsibility had fallen on me. My brother-in-law was working, but all the bills were on me because he was not helping out and Calvin was not working. I worked for the school district full-time and got a part time job at Ryan's Restaurant. I wanted to make a better life for my family so I started school, full-time, Monday through Friday to become a medical assistant. Four months short of completing school, I had a nervous breakdown and had to move back to South Carolina with my parents. Even then my stream of income from the school district, it was all we had coming in once a month because my husband was more interested in cheating and riding around s than finding a job, being a father to his children, or a real provider for his family.

How much can one take? It was June 2003 and Calvin was still not working. Instead, he plotted with my brother on the internet at night while I slept. They were online with women. My husband came up with a story of going to Texas with his dad and work, so he could provide for his family. Then I found out after paying my mom hundreds of dollars for collect calls he made, to discover he lived with another woman in Little Rock, Arkansas. Now, you want to talk about heartbroken, I was.

He was my high school sweetheart, we had problems over the years, we moved away to start over and save our marriage, but we also learned bad habits do die hard. The same thing happened again! He was not only cheating, but he lived with the woman he cheated on me with. When he came home to visit, he stole her clothes to bring me as gifts he purchased for me, but would lie and tell me he'd purchased the things just for me. This stuff blew my mind. I was completely bewildered. How could someone I loved so much treat me this way? How could we go through so much together, and this is the appreciation I get? I would never treat any person this way, no matter what might have happen. I loved my husband but I've reached my breaking point and I just couldn't put up with him anymore.

The children and I moved. Calvin came to visit, or called saying he was on the bus and needed to be picked up, but I later found out his mistress would drop him off and he'd walk to my house. I spend so much time chasing a relationship with him which was non-existent. I took him back because I wanted to believe he was really going to change. I was desperate, and gullible of every word falling from his conniving lips. He was very convincing when he expressed his love for me. I fell for it, but it was all a lie. Time after time he did the same thing. Finally, I was tired of being hurt and I told him I was done. All of this continued for months and then suddenly, he was back at his mom's house for good. It's possible his mistress got a taste of her own medicine. Maybe she got tired of the lies.

Calvin would call me and use the children to get next to me. At the time, I fell prey to all the foolishness because honestly, I still loved him. Even after all these years, and all he's put me through, I still had great affection for him. When he called, he'd ask me to come to his mom's house in Sumter, and like a fool I went, hoping and praying we could work on our marriage and be together again. I hoped we could be the family we'd talked about for years. He always made me believe we could make it because we were Calvin and Rochelle (Greta)! I let him come over for family day and I imagined change.

However, a couple of months later he was staying over at my house. He got up in the middle of the night to leave and it's when I decided it was over, we were done. It was 2004 and I was finally at the point I was done and would never return to a life with him. My heart was ready to be mended and healed from all of the hurt, shame, and abuse of this marriage. I endured it because to me marriage was a sacred vow before the Lord to remain as one.

CALLING IT QUITS
Chapter Seven

In 2004, I wondered what would come next. I still was not over the marriage, but my heart was finished with that life. I started to heal and love myself, but it was easier said than done. For a while I was getting back on track spiritually. Even though I went through all of this, I'd been a minister of the Gospel since 1999. So, all of this showed me God had a mission, work, and plan for me. How would I minister to others with all I went through? I started reading my Word more and studying to show myself approved. I buried myself in God's Word; I fasted and prayed expecting God would redeem the time and propel me to where I should be at this time in my life. I was off-track with God because of all the other things happening. I made a vow to God I would never let anyone else pull me from Him. I would never let anyone take me to another barren place again. I was on a mission to serve God and give Him my all. I got a mentor and moved further into my calling. I'm not saying God became important because I was not with my husband anymore. God was always important, I always served Him nonstop.

By 2005, I did well, working in ministry, and walking

in my calling. My leaders decided it was time for me to be ordained. March of 2005 I was ordained as an elder in the Lord's Church and Working Missions. I was a prophetic intercessor and had a prophetic call on my life, but because of all I had endured, I was unsure if it was what I wanted.

Now I was ready to revisit divorce actions so I reached out to Calvin to ask for the divorce. He sent messages to me saying I was not called to preach, I was nobody, and he would not sign the divorce papers. I spent over a thousand dollars trying to get a divorce but with no success.

Oe day I took my kids to the library to get some books. While there, I started talking to my mom's friend who worked there. Somehow, we got on the subject of divorce and she showed me a book. She told me to print the divorce decree template from the book and have someone help me fill it out completely and correctly and file it with the courts. I found a lady who helped me complete and notarize the form for $150. I took the paperwork to family court, and paid the fees. The papers were sent to Calvin and he had 30 days to respond. He never responded so they sent me a court date and I appeared with my witness. The judge granted me my divorce and full custody of my children. While in session he asked me if I wanted alimony and I said no. I only wanted to be free of the heartache, pain, and suffering. I just wanted to move on with my life.

Not only did the judge give me all I wanted, he also allowed me to retain the use of my last name. I did not want to go through the stress of completing another load of paperwork to have my name changed.

At the end of the court session, the judge told me the decree was usually mailed but if I waited about thirty minutes, he would make sure I received the decree that day. Even though I was overwhelmed by all of the events of the day, there was still a part of me which was still messed up, hurt, and broken.

HAUNTED BY THE PAST
Chapter Eight

A few weeks went by, and Gretta, my alter ego, started convincing me to do things I should not be doing. My past came back to haunt me. The void in me needed what I didn't want to give it; especially since I was a child of God, active in ministry, and a mother, I tried to stay focused, but I found myself being with men again. I let the enemy have his way with me. I lived a double life. In front of people, I hid the fact I was flirtatious and very loose. I was fornicating and talking to other women's husbands. Yes, ashamed, I did the same thing to some woman's husband, some woman did to me. Who was I hurting? Me, Did I care? Did Gretta care? The thing which hurt the most is these men cared nothing for me, we were each other's temporary fixes. I was an easy target, and they could tell I was trying to fill a void. Despite all I did, I never brought men home around my children. They never saw me leaving or coming in, nor did they ever experienced neglect from me. No matter what I did, my children always came first because I was the only parent they had.

While with men I barely knew, I told them about my terrible childhood; how I was raped and molested by family members, and raped by a stranger. To them, this story seemed to be the perfect recipe for disaster, making me effortless prey. They would say the magic words to get what they wanted and then go back to their wives. I would be left alone over and over again. Gretta kept telling me they really did want me, but deep within I knew they were using me. No problem: I used them too.

A few months later I started dating a man much older than me. He treated me nicely, communicated with me, and did things for me. I soon learned he had another woman in a different state and so I let him go.

Not long after this relationship, I started dating a man who lived in a different town from me, but we talked all day. He would not do anything with me in public. Even though I knew the relationship would not go far, I started developing feelings for him and he claimed he felt the same about me. Months and months went by and it just felt like nothing had changed so we agreed to just remain friends and I cut the sex out of the relationship.

One day I was minding my own business, and a phone call came through with some information exposing me and exposing Gretta.. What was I going to do? How would I show my face? I knew I needed to check myself and get it together because I didn't want my children to hear anything about their mom in the streets.

I stopped running around and just concentrated on my job and my children. I, once again went back to God. I fasted and prayed, asking God to restore me and make me a pure vessel for Him. I got back into God's Word doing my rituals of fasting two to three days a week, I asked God for forgiveness. I also proclaimed His word, "A man who finds a wife finds a good thing."

I realized I could not do the Lord's job, so patiently I waited on Him. I have to admit this was the most difficult feat of my life. Waiting is NOT fun either. I was very lonely. I questioned why all this crazy stuff was happening to me. I wondered why I couldn't be loved and treated like a woman. Why did my marriage have to end? Why was I the only one alone? No one saw the hurt, the pain, and the brokenness I was feeling. Again, I just wanted to die. I did many things to try to take my life. I overdosed on pills. I tried to drive off the side of a bridge. I even contemplated slicing my own wrist. I was faithless and hopeless. I did not realize it was all in God's plan to anoint me even the more and prepare me for the call on my life.

In the back of my mind, I wondered what would come next. From a little girl there seemed to be a battle lurking around the corner, so, I cringed as I waited on the next battle. Slowly but surely, the next attack moved in. I just didn't recognize it would come through my son, Matt.

DYSFUNCTIONAL FAMILY
Chapter Nine

When I thought I was doing the best I could as a single mother to hold the family together because my husband left his family. Why had I become the blame for the family falling apart? My son Matt blamed me early on for his dad leaving. He had his own set of demons following him because of our dysfunction. He, as I, were closet emotionalists. I was devastated to discover his plot to hurt me. He said he was mad because I wouldn't let his dad come back home. His line of questioning and line of reasoning was righteous indignation, while he wanted to hear nothing of the struggle I shielded him from. He said he understood, but he didn't. He was as I, desired the look and feel of a family unit, though it was far gone. He suffered silently so long without ever a mention, and thought he could solve his problem by conspiring to kill his mother. He was venting by acting out. When Matt was 13, he pulled all of his clothes out of the closet and threatened to run away to his dad. No matter what was said, he thought everything was my fault. He said he would keep a knife with him, and threatened I may not wake up if I went to sleep. It is very unnerving to hear a threat from your child, but I prayed God would let us both live. Without badgering him, I just wanted him to see we all had problems and I tried my best to hang on. No matter whose fault it was, at some point we were all at fault.

I did not give up on helping him understand what really happened. The breakup was very hard for me, but sorely devastating for the children. They all had a great relationship with their dad. He spent time with them, did many things with them, and showed them much love, so I understood why they were hurt by our flawed relationship which led to the family's breakup. Of course, Matt took it the hardest. The gap a boy feels as he grows into a man without the model in his own dad gave our son a complete meltdown. He looked up to his dad and now he was gone.

Everyone knows there is the truth, and three sides to the truth. Your truth, the other person's truth, and what really happened. Calvin told the children on many occasions his perspective, leaving it to appear I was the bad one. In the meantime, hearing only his perspective, Matt could not handle it. He became belligerent and unruly. He showed his contempt for me more and more. I asked Calvin to relieve the children by visiting more, or let them live with him for a spell, but he chose to go back to Little Rock, Arkansas without ever dealing with it. He made promises, but never followed through with any of them. In defense of my children's hurt, I asked him to please stop making promises he didn't plan to keep to the kids.

My daughter, Ala questioned me about her dad's ability to keep his promises, and Matt never let me forget the blame of our messed up family, the perfection of his dad doing nothing I claimed he did. Matt transferred those perceptions (lies) to his sister. He affirmed to her I pushed their dad away and would not let him come around or let them talk to him. I heard Matt one night telling his sister I would not even let them go to their other grandmother's house. The truth of the matter was I used to cry wondering why she would pass our house to see her youngest son's children and not ever come to see these children. She would not call them. I was infuriated by her lack of fellowship, I was bothered and completely annoyed because these were still her grandchildren.

I often thought about the comment she made to my mom on the church ground at the beginning of our relationship, I was not good enough for her son; but who was the one unfaithful and not true to his marriage? Surely not me I was committed to the end.

I continued my church relationship. I worked long hours, did fun things with my children, and yes I pushed myself to have fun with my sisters. With all these activities, I was still null and void inside, and brokenness was building more and more every day. I took on the belief of my son and blamed myself for everything happening at this point. "God, why? Am I cursed?" Why did I have to keep experiencing the same things over and over?", I asked the Lord. I believed something horrible was spoken over me or this was just my past coming back to haunt me. I did not have a perfect past, but no one does. The enemy was out to destroy me, bring me down in shame, fear, hurt, and brokenness. I kept telling myself daily we all fall short and must get up, dust ourselves off, and move on. However, for me, because I never really loved myself, I just thought I got the worst of things. My past issues were now coming back hard to haunt me.

Through all the devastations of my family, my life, and my body, I received a phone call from the doctor who ordered my last battery of tests. He informed me the tests showed a spot in my small intestines, and was cancerous, and I needed treatment immediately. "Lord, another thing?" This is all so insurmountable. It seemed all hell broke loose. I had to call my pastor for counsel. I knew my pastor didn't have my feelings, but I wanted him to know I did not want to have any kind of treatment. I did not want to die and leave my children with no mother, especially since their dad was gone. I fasted and prayed and asked God what I should do. I wanted to live to declare the works of the Lord. After a three day fast with prayer, I told the doctor I would take the chemo regiment, which required me to take pills, but Chemotherapy was totally out of the question. Two weeks later, I started the regiment for six weeks. I then had to be retested before surgery to cut a small piece of my small intestines off where the cancer cells were found.

After recovery from surgery, I was scared to talk to anybody about my decision not to do Chemo, because I was afraid I might have made the wrong choice. When I returned for another procedure to examine the inside of the incision, the only thing the doctors could find was scar tissue. I was healed of stomach cancer of which many people die from. I trusted God and He healed me again. Even though it was a long recovery, I kept trusting and believing God and proclaiming His word I shall live and not die.

This was just the tip of the iceberg, so many things were going on in my body and it seemed a lot of the stuff started appearing after the separation from my husband. I asked myself, "What's next?"

I felt in my bones something else near tragic was headed my way. I was the deli manager at Food Lion in our hometown and we all were notified the store would be closing. This meant I had to find another job. I would lose my insurance and I really needed income to take care of my children and me. Thank God I was transferred to a store in Monks Corner. I commuted an hour and a half each way, every day.

* * * * * * * * *

Another day another battle. Ala, who was about 11 years old, started having behavior problems at school and was very depressed. She was writing notes in school she wanted to kill herself. The first time I was called to the school, the counselor only told me she was concerned with her mood and how she seemed distant, and not responding to the teachers. About two weeks later, I was called to the school again because Ala attempted to take her life. I talked to her at the school and when I got home from work, we talked again. I wanted to find out what was bothering her, and she admitted she missed her dad and she felt like he did not love her anymore. She said he loved someone else's children and had abandoned her and her brother.

"Why, mom?" she asked, me. "Why would he leave us and go to another family?" I tried my best to answer her questions without blaming him. I prayed in hopes she would be ok, and she seemed to be. However, the next day her brother called me at work saying I needed to come home because he found Ala in the room trying to hang herself with a belt. She said she did not want to live anymore because she could not have her dad and her family back the way it had always been. What was I going to do? My baby needed help and I didn't know how to help her.

Knowing something had to be done, I just swallowed my pride and called around to get my daughter the help she needed. The next day I went to the school and they referred her to mental health for counseling, three days a week. Even though it might have looked odd to others, I knew this was what my daughter needed. After I found out my insurance would cover her visits we started right away. I was willing to take her for as long as she needed to go. After about three weeks of intense counseling they decided she was better. Even though we had to take one day at a time, they were convinced Ala would make a full recovery.

Slowly but surely, she was coping and getting better every day. I still watched her because I was very scared of a set back and prayed she would be ok. Weeks turned into months and soon she was good. She accepted the fact her dad was not coming back home. Although he had the opportunity to be their father, he chose to walk out of their lives. The thing hurt more than losing my husband and my best friend was his mother acted as if my children didn't exist. Her neglect hurt them to the core so I tried my best not to make a big deal out of her blatant neglect because I did not want to make my children sad.

While I stayed focused on my children and the ministry, I still had a big void in my life. I was also very vulnerable. On the outside, I appeared fine. I talked to men and tried dating, but on the inside I was falling apart. I began to unleash the hurt from my marriage onto every man who showed interest in me. I knew it would be impossible for me to have a successful relationship if I didn't get rid of the hurt and pain. I knew I had to release the pain and let it go.

My health was not great. I saw many different doctors for many different diagnoses, and at the same time I blamed myself for everything which happened in my life; even the things I had no control over. You could say, I was a glutton for punishment.

I said, "Lord please just take me now!" My destructive spirit has attached itself to my daughter. She claimed the same evil spirit which tormented me. When I heard my child say she wanted to die, it made me have the same emotion. I did not want to live, or even exist. I didn't have strength or faith to face any of this stuff. Why? Because it was my entire fault and t nothing I could do to help my plight.

I started treatment for the sickness sometime later, and I got worse instead of better. My blood pressure spiked so high that I was sent to a nephrologist for treatment. I was on six different prescriptions for blood pressure, including a patch, but the medicines were not controlling my blood pressure. The doctor advised I should stop working for a while. I applied for the medical leave. During the application process, I found I had short- and long-term disability. I was entitled to receive short term disability for 121 days and long-term disability for up to 24 months. What a blessing

ALL THE WAY IN
Chapter Ten

I was now home and made the choice to catch up on my Biblical studies. The benefits of hanging out in the Word of God could keep me hidden, focused, and sane. Well let me interject, experience will never keep you. I was tempted with phone calls for some of my male friends. Marty in particular took up a lot of my time. My loneliness led me back in a relationship with a man from my past... Marty was a pastor from Charleston, S.C.

I believed because I was in God's Word more, had a Christian companion, and things were better with my children, I would be happy, and our lives would get back on track.

But out of nowhere, my Matt came at me again with his torment; lashing out and blaming me for not letting his dad come back into my life. I simply told him my relationship with his dad had nothing to do with his relationship with his dad. Nothing I did or said changed his mind. I was the bad person in his mind. He was never content with anyone I related to.

It took approximately five months for Matt to accept any relationship with a man friend. He slowly accepted his dad was not coming back. Then his feelings changed to anger and contempt. He wanted nothing to do with him from this point.

After the hurdle of him releasing his relationship with his dad, and not having to defend myself about the failed relationship, I could feel more comfortable with Marty. I cautiously allowed him to enter my children's lives. Ala was more forthcoming than Matt about my dating choices.. She and Marty established a good relationship. When my son saw how close they had become, he slowly developed a distant relationship with Marty. He was careful to get too close. I was happy he let him in at all.

Our relationship was growing and I yielded my heart towards Marty bit by bit. A year had practically passed and I was on a joy kick because of Marty's and my relationship, ministry, my children, and everything else. This could be it: the makings for a happy life. I started helping with his personal ministry. The next thing you know, he asked for my hand in marriage with a beautiful ring.

I spent a good bit of time traveling to Charleston to

help Marty in his pastoral ministry. He saw my
diligence and appointed me co-pastor and gave my
own office. He gave me several duties in
administration and in the worship experience.
Though moving pretty fast, things were going well;
for a while.

Some time had passed and I was to host a three-day
birthday celebration for Marty at the church. His
uncle was to be guest speaker for the three nights.
The first two nights went extremely well, but the final
night didn't end well at all.

I got to Charleston early on Tuesday. I met with
Marty and we went to lunch at one of our regular
Chinese places. As we were sitting down to eat,
something seemed off to me, but Marty reassured me
everything was ok.

When we got back in the car, I reached into the arm
rest to get a piece of tissue for my nose. When I
realized his ex-wife had been in the car, and had been
going through my insurance papers. Yes, Marty's car
was insured under my insurance company.

I spent several hours decorating the church, buying
food, and decorating a special cake.

I was ambushed the final night in the worst way. I was disrespected as acting co-pastor by some comments made from the pulpit and one of the visitors was Marty's former wife.

When church ended, I was out of there. I refused to hang around. I did not return the following Sunday nor did I feel compelled to come to the week-long revival. I did not go the first night. I received a phone call from Marty, my fiancé on Tuesday inquiring why didn't I attend church on Sunday and Monday for revival. I let him know I would be there Tuesday night and the rest of the week.

On this night after arriving to the church, I went to my office and noticed my picture was gone from my desk. I asked Marty about the picture and he said no one had been in my office; it turned out to be a lie. The ex-wife had taken my picture and I believe he knew she had taken it.

I did stay for service and I did praise and worship and presided as well.

What came next was heartbreaking and all I could do

was sit there and act as if nothing had happened. Upon closing out that night there was no recognition or respect given to me at all. I still smiled, hugged, and shook the hands of our guest.

Pastor never said anything else to me, so I left and did not return. I later found out he and his ex-wife had gotten back together. I didn't even get a call to inquire about why I did not go back to church for the rest of the revival or even Sunday for any matter.

Next Monday I was sick in bed, and I didn't receive a phone call or anything from my so-called fiancé. So, I decided to reach out to him and ask what was going on with them. He told me he did not know what he wanted, so I decided for him and called off the entire relationship, which was ministry and marriage.

He tried to talk to me several times but I was not going to go down the road again. I decided I was not taking any more mental abuse from any man, and especially one that I was not married to. I could have dropped the car immediately from my insurance, have his phone disconnected and get my computer from the church, but I didn't. I did, however, warn him that he had until the end of the month to get him some insurance on his car.

That was the end of that for me, but emotionally I was tied to him. He was another man I let into my heart and again, I was hurt. Whose fault was this? Was this what I deserved again? Was I that bad of a person that I did not deserved to be loved and respected?

Although it took months, I allowed God to heal my heart, but still felt abused. I was exposed again, thrown to the slander, put to shame and left alone again. What's wrong with Gretta? She did not come to my rescue this time.

SAILING ON BROKEN PIECES
Chapter Eleven

All I wanted to do was run as far and as fast as I could away from this futile moment. I felt like an "oops." Why was I created and chosen? I heard and believed the rhetoric because of the results of my life; at least in my finite estimation, it provided all the negative outcome people said.

My grandma was a shero to me. She got me. She understood me, my dreams, and my feelings. She taught me many things and with a third-grade education, she was not hindered in her information and wisdom. She was fair with me. When I messed up, she gave me the hardest time and correction, but on the flip side, she also encouraged me and told me never to give up.

I tried using every broken piece of my life to get to the next place, praying and hoping life would get better.

I moved to Atlanta again. This time I was determined it was going to be God first, then my children. I wanted a fresh start. My family and I really needed that. I wanted to get myself together, starting with my heart.

Kierra was there for college, and Matt and Ala were starting a new school. Yes, I said I had my children with me, and you might be wondering why Kierra was mentioned. Remember, she is my biological sister who moved to Atlanta with me the first time in 1999. My parents signed her over to me so I would enroll her in school. yes she was my dependent too.

We were expecting a great reward in Atlanta because the last few years had been challenging. I just wanted everything in my life to be different and better.

At first because I was on long term disability, my plan was to be a stay-at- home mom, help Kierra with college and find us a great ministry to join. However, being a stay at home mom greatly affected me. That life was not for me only because I was used to working and getting out.

I started looking for jobs on the internet and completing applications for employment. My background was mostly in management and supervising with customer service and food service experience. I also had a healthcare background and experience in the medical field, I really enjoyed customer service and food service.

One Tuesday I submitted an application for a food service supervisor and the very next day someone reached out to me from the Atlanta International Airport about a supervisor's job. I went to the interview and was offered the job the very same day.

Before leaving, I told the interviewer I needed to think about the opportunity. I communicated if I was going to accept the job, I would show up the next day to start my process with all the other hired associates. I wanted to make sure I made the right choice, a job or disability. I had a lot to consider

Upon arriving home, my intention was to talk with my three children to find out how they felt about me starting work after moving to a new place. I just knew that they would be dead against me going back to work. Instead, they encouraged me to get back into the work field again. Even Kierra was all for me going back to work. She even volunteered to help out more until school started.

Looking back, I blame myself for Kierra not going to school like she'd planned. Shortly after I started work, she decided to get a job until school started. However, when it was time to start school at Clark Atlanta, she gave me an excuse that she would start another semester and work to save some money so she would be able to pay her part in bills and pay for the car that I had gotten for her.

Kierra got to know people far quicker than I and she started getting into things and spending more time planning her work life instead of going to college. I felt like it was my fault because even though she was grown, I felt like I should have stepped up more to make sure she did what was necessary at that time in her life.

IN THE CITY NOW
Chapter Twelve

One of the first people we met was a young lady who lived at the front of the building and her name was Lena. From the beginning we knew she was a sweetheart, but we also knew that she had problems with drugs and alcohol and she had a newborn baby. From day one we were connected to Lena and her baby. She had a live-in boyfriend, but she was not faithful to him because he was much older than she was and he knew that she often sold her body for drugs, alcohol, and money.

I became more connected to her at first, because the girl had a passion like me. She could cook, she was clean, and she took care of her son. Her live-in boyfriend was not the biological father to her son, but financially, he stood in the gap and took care of them. I used to talk to Lena and try to get her to understand that she had a newborn baby and she had someone who at least cared about her. I told her the drugs and alcohol were going to cause her a lot of trouble. I would see her take her baby in those streets all times of night. I often offered to watch him for a few hours for her to go out and just be able to breathe, and at the same time know that her baby was safe because he was in my care.

We also got to know the other tenants in the building. One of the main tenants we met was from upstairs and that's how our Atlanta life really got started. Everyone connected and we used to have a blast.

Since I was the main cook in the building, we'd all get together, mainly at my house and cook, eat and play cards. What started out to be something every so often turned into almost an everyday thing and that was when I met Mitchell. Later, I found out he was invited to the house to meet someone else, but from day one his eyes were set on me, and that's how our story began Mitchell and I started off very slow because I did not want to get hurt again. I did not want to rush into a serious relationship. However, his thoughts about a relationship were much different from mine. He said he saw who he wanted, and it was love at first sight. Mitchell did have a few issues, smoked blacks and weed.

He was not the type of person I was used to, nor was I used to that lifestyle. . My first husband smoked blacks from time to time, but never around me.

Mitchell was way more aggressive than my first husband or any of the other men I ever dated. In the beginning I had my hard wall of protection up, but he kept saying He knew what he wanted and he worked hard to get it. I could not push him away so easily. He was adamant on not going anywhere. I would just stare at him with an attitude as I pretended to ignore him.

Weeks went by and he kept pursuing me. I was impressed because he also held a job, something my ex-husband never did. Mitchell came around mostly on weekends at first, then he started showing up every day. He was definitely persistent.

When we finally became a couple, my youngest daughter, Ala was extremely happy about it because she adored Mitchell, and he adored her. Ala was his baby and that was great for me because not only did I deserve happiness, but my children deserved to be happy as well. My son had a very hard time adapting to any man trying to come into my life. Mitchell, on the other hand, suffered because he really adored all of my children.

I worked a whole lot and the weeks grew into months so quickly. Our relationship was also growing.

We had been in a relationship a year and I thought I was in a secure place with him. Although I was happy, thoughts of my past relationships I thought, "This is too good to be true! What's lurking around the corner? When is the next big hurricane going to hit and destroy everything?

One morning as I got up for work, Mitchell was sleeping hard and his phone was ringing. I didn't think it strange, because he was often late for work. His alarm kept going off, so when I got out of the shower and got dressed. I tried to wake him but he was not moving. I picked up the phone to turn off the alarm and noticed he had six messages from a woman who sent him pictures. She was naked in some of the pictures. I just froze, because for a moment I could not believe what I was looking at.

I sat the phone down and continued to get dressed and drove myself to work. I left Mitchell there, still asleep, knowing when he woke up he would not have a way to get to work. In the moment, I didn't care what he would think, I just couldn't get those pictures out of my mind.

I could not worry about Mitchell right then because I had three stores to run. All my attention needed to be on my job. I was supposed to get off at 3 p.m. because I was the morning manager. However, the night manager had an emergency and needed someone to cover the shift. I volunteered to stay to close so I didn't get off until 10 p.m. I didn't care about the long day because I knew, sooner or later, I would have to go home to face my issues with Mitchell. I was in no hurry to get home because I just didn't want to deal with the drama.

In my mind I lost another fight and I didn't have enough strength to go through it anymore. So, when I got home, Mitchell was not there yet because on Tuesdays he and his best friend went out for two-dollar drinks, so Tuesdays, were late nights for him.

I knew the situation with him would not be pretty. We talked every day at work and he did not call me once. When he got home, I was in bed, but not asleep. He took his shower and tried easing into the bed because I was a very easy person to wake. As soon as he put his head on the pillow, I got up and asked him if there was anything he needed to tell me. Well of course he said, "What are you talking about?"

I wanted to scream, yell, and just push him out of the window, but in a soft voice I just said, "Don't play with me."

I had to be up in about two hours for work because I had to be on my concourse at my store by 3 a.m. I needed to leave home by 2:15 a.m. so I went to bed. I thought to myself, this man really thinks I'm crazy.

The next morning he got up to take me to work. The first five minutes were quiet. Then he had the nerve to ask me why I took the car the previous day and left him home sleeping? At this point, all hell broke loose. I let him have it. Mitchell had all kinds of excuses, and he even blamed me because he said I had no business going through his phone. I could not believe he blamed me for something he got caught doing!

This man had asked me to marry him. Our phones had never been private before. In fact, on many occasions, he'd ask me to answer his phone. Now, suddenly, he said I was snooping. I was done! I refused to be treated like that again. My husband played me but I was not going to get played again!

For days he begged and pleaded with me but I would

not listen to anything he had to say. I'd made up my mind, but then the old self-blaming spirit had come back to haunt me again, telling me I caused it; it was my fault.

Mitchell continued begging me to take him back as he swore he had never cheated on me. He said he never asked the girl to send the pictures to his phone. He claimed they were friends before I came along. He said she had never done anything like that before. Of course, I didn't believe that foolishness. However, when you feel weak, alone, abandoned, and unloved, you will settle for things you shouldn't settle for.

It took some time for me to come around, but gradually I allowed him to come back.

Things seemed to be working out for my family. Then someone broke into our house. Kierra and Matt went back to South Carolina, but Ala and I moved to Decatur, Ga. About two weeks after we moved someone was murdered in the building we'd just moved to.

Mitchell and I were not doing good and I just wanted to get out. I moved back to South Carolina for a week, before I realized Atlanta was where I wanted to be. We went back to Atlanta and moved in with Mitchell's best friend for a little while, before moving in with one of my employees.

We lived in Stone Mountain, GA, which was 53 miles to work, one way. I had a long distance to travel so I moved into a house closer to work.

Shortly after the move, my health got worse. I had Multiple Myeloma and Ala, who was pregnant at the time, was experiencing health issues as well. I Take care of my daughter. One day my oncologist told me going to college and working was too much on my body and I really needed to be around family who could help me get through this cancer and help with my daughter.

Being in Atlanta without family was not safe for us so I had to make some hard choices. So, we decided to move back to South Carolina for good.

STILL SURVIVING
Chapter Thirteen

I endured so many years of sickness, problems, test, trials, ins and outs, but with God's help I am still surviving.

In 2011, I started over again. . I felt like someone else lived inside my body, mind, and soul. How did I get here, and why was I going through the same thing, over and over again? I still tried to make the best of my life.

Kierra lived with a roommate in a two-bedroom unit, She said Ala and I could come live with her. We made the best of a tough situation.

Two months later of August 2011, we moved into our own house. I got a job by then and we were headed in the right direction and there was no turning back.

I had friends, but no relationships. I dived into church and got involved in as much things as I could. I battled with Post Traumatic Stress Disorder (PTSD), but who was I going to tell?

I knew I needed to find doctors in South Carolina, especially an oncologist so I could keep up with the treatments. My family was unaware of my treatments. It was easier to hide when I lived in Atlanta.

Ala was experiencing a high-risk pregnancy so she needed an obstetrician immediately. Life was stressful because I had so much to do. However, I did not want to be back in South Carolina nor did I want to be near Kierra because I was still hurt by the way things ended in Atlanta. I loved her but there were just some things I could not get past and maybe she felt the same. We never spoke about what happened in Atlanta and I told myself I'll get over it, but it tore me up inside.

After all these years, of hurt, anger, betrayal, and not feeling loved made me feel like I was exploding. I kept asking myself what would be next. Who would be next? What or who would I destroy next? Was I that bad? I did not have answers to those questions. I just continued to blame myself for all the bad things which happened to me.

All the cares of the world seemed to weigh on my shoulders and I felt like I was at my breaking point and I had no one to talk to. Who would want to even listen to me? All I could do was cry out to God. Maybe he would love me enough to come to my rescue. He was all I had. Don't get me wrong, I trusted God and I knew He heard my prayers.

I was working full time, Ala was in school, and Matt was living with us too. Matt had left Atlanta not long after Kierra to live with my parents in Manning. He was still battling with massive Hydronephrosis of his right Kidney and was in and out of the hospital. He also had surgery to treat the problem. Many times, I had to travel from Atlanta because he had been admitted to the Medical University of South Carolina, in Charleston. After all these years we were still dealing with the same issue of his right kidney not functioning properly. He will undergo reconstructive surgery to fix the problem.

I had a lot on me. Matt battled kidney disease, I battled cancer, and Kierra and Ala were pregnant. With everything going on, we still loved each other and we supported each other.

In 2011, I worked at a call center and working at Food Lion, part-time. I wanted to make as much money as I could, while I was able. I had so many health issues and I didn't know how long I would be able to work. I didn't work the two jobs for long before my doctors were telling me to file for disability because they wanted me to restart chemotherapy for Multiple Myeloma. Deep down inside I was screaming for help, but I still tried to be strong for my children.

I was very concerned because Ala, who was 15 years old, was about to deliver a baby. It was a lot to take in. How were we going to pay the high rent, utilities, and all the other bills? How would we make ends meet? Although Kierra was worked full-time, she was also pregnant, and Matt was being who he was.

I believed part of him hated me. He lashed out about everything. I could hardly talk to him about anything. He hung out with the wrong crowd. He dropped out of school with a total disrespect for me.

It seemed the more I tried; the more things were went wrong. Although I wore a smile on the outside, when I'd go to my room and lay across my bed, my pillow would be wet with tears. I used sex to keep my mind off my problems. I didn't have a steady friend, but I had a few partners. Once again, my problems pushed me back to my old ways.

October 2, 2011, Ala had to be induced so she would have her daughter. The baby's dad and granddad came from Atlanta to be there when she was born. Since labor was slow, I went home with plans of returning early the next morning, but told them to call me if her labor progressed. I received an emergency phone call around 1 p.m. the next day her labor had progressed and she needed an epidural because her blood pressure was through the roof.

I suggested she have the baby naturally because I didn't believe in epidurals. It was what my grandmother taught me and I passed it down to both of my girls. However, the nurse told her differently, so when I arrived at the hospital, she was waiting for the anesthesiologist to come and give her the epidural. When she got the epidural, she was already 10 centimeters and it was time to push. Before long, I had my very first grandchild. I was the happiest person in the world. She was the reason I fought through my health issues. She gave me another reason to live. I often felt like I failed my own children, but I fought hard to be a better grandmother. I wanted my children and now my granddaughter to know I was there for them and I would never leave them.

When we got home, motherhood seemed to come

naturally for Ala. She did a good job caring for her baby. Almost seven months later, we were in the hospital again because it was time for Kierra to have her baby. On April 25, 2012, Kierra had her baby girl naturally and she appreciated the experience. However, the baby arrived six weeks early and experienced some health issues. I was there for my children and grandchildren.

As time went by we moved to Cayce, SC. It was a different area for us so we had to meet new people. . By this time Matt was expecting his first son. Avery was born on August 28, 2014.

Days turned into months and months turned into a few years. In May 2015 we moved into a bigger home, because finally, after five years, I got my disability and was able to help out financially. Things were going pretty good for us. This time when we moved, we didn't take Matt with us. I felt like it was time for him to stand on his own and be a man. Parting with him hurt all of us, but it was time for him to stand on his own.

Matt, his girlfriend, and their son moved into their own apartment. He was distant from us for a while but eventually, he came back around. I will never forget. It was Christmas 2015 and the celebration was at my house. My parents came up for a few days to spend Christmas with us. Matt came and it felt so good to have all of my children together again. I was glad to be in my son's life again.

Life would have been even better if my former significant other would have been there. He walked away in November. On October 3, 2015, on my oldest granddaughter's birthday, South Carolina got hit with a major flood and many things had to be cancelled or rescheduled, including my planned and paid for wedding. While we recovered from the flood, he just vanished. That really hurt me. This was a man who said he wanted to spend the rest of his life with me. Yes, it hurt for a long time. Since I did not have an explanation for his disappearance, I blamed myself. I was so frustrated. I deserved to know why he walked out on me.

WHAT'S NEXT
Chapter Fourteen

Nearly three months later, the most tragic thing happened to our family. We got a phone call on Saturday, January 5, 2016, mom was in the emergency room in Sumter, South Carolina. Although I had plans to attend a CD release, I had to miss it and rush down to see what was going on with my mom. Upon arriving at the hospital, I found out mom was admitted for an infection in her foot and her glucose level was very high. Later on, the E.R. doctor told us mom had a very bad gangrene infection, and it was shutting down her kidneys, causing her sugar levels to be high. We were told an orthopedic surgeon would come in the next morning to view everything with her and decide what needed to be done.

I stayed with her and the next morning the surgeon gave us news which changed our lives. Mom needed a debridement surgery to remove the damage and infected tissue. The surgery was scheduled for that morning. We were told the plan might change once they got her to surgery and could fully assess the damage. Unfortunately, after accessing mom's condition, the surgeon told us parts of mom's feet needed to be amputated and he need our permission to perform the surgery.

Once the surgery was over the doctors came and talked to us. Someone had to tell mom. My dad was not a very strong person when it came to things like this. Being the oldest child, I had to put all my tears on the back burner and be strong for mom. Once we got in her room, everybody but me froze up, so I had to break the news to mom. How could I be strong enough for the entire family? How could I look my mom in her face and tell her some of her toes were already gone and they would need to do many more surgeries to get to the healthy tissue to give her a chance to live healthy again. This was too much; it was extremely hard enough to look at her in the hospital because I was usually the one looking up from the hospital bed.

Mom was always pretty healthy. She'd never faced a major health crisis. I looked her in the eyes and simply told her this was not how her story was going to end. I assured her she was going to get through all of this and encouraged her to be positive. I told her she would not die from this. Deep on the inside I wanted to just break, but quitting was not an option for her or for us.

After 11 surgeries and being hospitalized for 33 days, my mom lost portions of both feet. We did get through the ordeal. Mom has recovered and is back at home and drives anywhere she wants to go.

* * * * * * * * * *

God proved himself over and over and His Word has gotten us through every trial and tribulation in my life. By the time mom was ready to go back to her home in Manning, we were all about to move, for the first time ever, into our own separate homes. This was a big challenge for me because I had never been separated from all of my children and grandchildren at the same time.

I wanted to move back to Atlanta, but when the time came for me to move, mom had a setback and needed me to take care of her. I had about two weeks to find some place to live because Kierra and Ala already had their places secured. At the minute, God proved himself again. I found a cottage just right for me, so I secured it and moved in on May 2, 2016.

I lived by myself and I felt lonely, depressed, and

bitter. I still helped take care of my mom, but she lived at Kierra's house. She used a wheelchair but her chair could not fit through all the doors in my house so she would not be able to stay with me. Because I was disabled and Kierra worked a full-time job, plus she was a college student with a young child, I felt the responsibility should rest mostly on me. I did things for her like appointments, paperwork and maintenance, I felt like it was too much on my sister/daughter.

I was so alone. This desperate and missing element was the thing which ignited and catapulted me to the next level. I decided to boost my business and really put Katie Pearls on the map. Katie Pearls is my cooking business birthed in me from a young girl, but I was always scared to step out because I was a very self-conscience person with low self-esteem.

One Saturday I had an idea while home in my bed. I sent Kierra a message to get some orders for dinners that Sunday. Surprisingly, I got 15 orders and it went very well. My menu was baked or BBQ chicken, rice and gravy, green beans and cornbread. Since the first dinner went so well, Katie Pearls sold dinners every week and sales grew more and more.

I got my first catering event and Katie Pearls took off and there was no turning back. Every week I did orders on Fridays or Sundays, depending on the days my customers wanted to order. I even started doing small family dinner orders, pies, cakes, and pasta meals.

Months went by and I was back into an old relationship with Marty, the pastor. We got married in August 2016, three years later, I wondered if I'd made another mistake. The decision to marry him three years ago seemed right, but was it now coming back to haunt me? Marty just up and left me. He moved back to Charleston. He sent a text message saying he was not coming back. He left me without any financial assistance. I was baffled. Should I just forget it all and try to mend my broken heart? I needed a lot of things mended and after 44 years I am still telling the stories of the good, the bad and the ugly.

A Pastor preached a sermon one Sunday and one of the nuggets from it really struck me. He said, "WHAT WAS MEANT TO HURT ME, SAVED MY LIFE." That statement felt so real for my life and seemed to be directed right at me.

Over all the years of hardship, sadness, happiness, hurt, sickness, disease, plots, maltreatment, cover ups, low self-esteem, etc., I look back at all the broken pieces of my life and wonder if I can use each and every one of those pieces to mend me. Can all these broken pieces from Gretta be used for God to get all the glory? There is a purpose and destiny for my life. I realize each broken piece can be used to mend Gretta back together.

At this time in my life I still feel like I'm being punished, being picked on, and going through so much, but who am I? Jesus gave his life for me, so who am I that I can't go through my trials.. God promised He would never leave or forsake us. He never promised people wouldn't forsake us.

I've learned people will never be able to treat me like God treats me and people will never be able to help me mend from the circumstances I have gone through. I often sit and think about the things I went through as a little girl and compare them to the things I go through now. Some are different and some are the same. I still sometimes feel like I'm not good enough because of my past.. I often feel like I have been left on an island alone with no food, clothes, or shelter and I am suffocating.

God knows I am far from perfect, but I know I am not what I use to be. I also know God is with me through every battle I face; He holds my hand. With God,I got this. I understand life a little better now. I see the road and I feel Him beside me, and God is going to use all my broken pieces and I will sail to the other side of this mountain without drowning or suffocating. To God be the Glory for all He has done, is doing and still going to do.

I am still surviving and I don't plan to give up.. Sometimes you are left on the journey alone and must understand some people can't always go where God is taking you. With God, all things are possible to them believe, and I totally believe God. His word is all the fight I have in me. I have been diagnosed with so my illness, diseases and sickness. God has brought me through every time.. The things kill some people, I am still battling and fighting everyday.

Some days my struggle is simply for strength to fight, not even for one more day, but for one more minute. God has been so good to me and has healed and delivered me so many times. When I was eleven years old, I was diagnosed with an intestinal virus. When I was thirteen years of age, I contracted Mononucleosis. By the time I was seventeen, I had to have my gallbladder removed. When I was seventeen,

I had my first miscarriage. When I was nineteen, I had my son and got married. When I was twenty-one, I had my daughter, lost another baby and had a hysterectomy. This same year I had major surgery on my right ankle from crushed bones. Right after that I had an aneurysms. In 2000 I was told that I was suffering from Fibromyalgia and also sent to a rheumatologist and treated for Rheumatoid Arthritis. In 2005, I was diagnosed with stomach cancer and a pulmonary embolism. In 2009 I was diagnosed with cancer again, Multiple Myeloma. In 2011, I was diagnosed with (HS) Hidradenitis Suppurativa, Plantar Fasciitis and Dystrophic Eczema. In 2015 I was also deemed disabled by the state of South Carolina and compensated for waiting since 2011. In 2001 I was tested and treated for joint dysfunction and degenerative joint disease. Then, I took a series of tests to find out that I was suffering from Multiple Sclerosis but was only going to be watched to see if treatment would be needed. In late 2017 I found out I needed treatment for Multiple Sclerosis. By this time it had progressed to the point where treatment was not work sufficiently. I was scanned again and was told the Multiple Myeloma was back again for the second time. So, what do I do? How do I handle all these life crises and diseases? I got so tired of surgeries, treatments, tests, exams, strategies, therapy, procedures, and a repeat of things that did not work because my body, mind, and soul were breaking down right before my very eyes. God was my only choice!

With all of this going on, I am here again, alone, fighting, confused, and full of every question I can think of; and it comes to me I am sailing on every broken piece of my life and it is taking me to the other side of the mountain. When it looked so dark and I felt like I fought in this life all alone, God reminded me He was and am still is right beside me and He will not leave me. So, I can see clearly now since most of the rain is gone, and I will continue to keep looking up to the hills from where my help comes from. We sometimes think help should come from family, friends, loved ones, and spouses. However, my help comes from the Lord and without him I would fail.

Over time, I have become stronger, but Gretta is still with me. She is a part of who I am. As life goes on, we will see how Gretta and I makes it. The two things I am sure of are God is always with me and with Him, I will always win!

ABOUT THE AUTHOR

Rhonda Whitaker -1975 is a native of South Carolina. She is the mother of three children and six grandchildren. She received a formal education in Clarendon School District #2 of SC and graduated with the distinguished class of 1993 from Manning High School.

Upon matriculating from high school Rhonda went on to pursue higher education and received her cosmetology and phlebotomy licensures. From an early age Rhonda had a very strong call on her life and received her ministerial license in November of 1999 and was ordained in March of 2005.

Rhonda is a woman of many gifts and is currently fulfilling multiple capacities. She is the owner and operator of *Katie Pearls This and That Foods* of Columbia SC, the visionary of *Unrevealed Gifts*, Whitaker is an actor, playwright, and an author. Rhonda's favorite Scripture is Psalm 91: 1, *"He that dwelleth in the secret place of the most high shall abide under the shadow of the Almighty."*

Rhonda believes she is called to minister to women who are wounded, broken, and abandoned. Her mission is to usher those women to a place of healing and full restoration.

www.ingramcontent.com/pod-product-compliance
Lightning Source LLC
Chambersburg PA
CBHW011141290426
44108CB00023B/2714